IMAGES OF WALES

TREFOREST,
GLYNTAFF AND RHYDYFELIN

On the Taff at Treforest

IMAGES OF WALES

TREFOREST,
GLYNTAFF AND RHYDYFELIN

RHODRI JOHN POWELL

TEMPUS

Frontispiece: On the Taff at Treforest.

First published 2005

Tempus Publishing Limited
The Mill, Brimscombe Port,
Stroud, Gloucestershire, GL5 2QG
www.tempus-publishing.com

British Library Cataloguing in Publication Data.
A catalogue record for this book is available from the British Library.

ISBN 0 7524 3507 8

Typesetting and origination by Tempus Publishing Limited.
Printed in Great Britain.

Contents

	Acknowledgements and Foreword	6
	Introduction	7
one	Treforest	9
two	The School of Mines	67
three	Treforest Industrial Estate	79
four	Glyntaff	93
five	Rhydyfelin	113

Acknowledgements

The author would like to thank the following for lending their valued photographs and for their help in compiling this book: John Batton, Anthony Evans, Mrs Freeguard, Royden Greening, Edwina Hawkins, Lyn Joshua, Betty Jones, David L. Jones, Walter Jones, Pat Lawrence, John Preece, David Russell, G. Way, Lyn Williams and the staff of Glyntaff crematorium.

A special thanks to the following for their time and patience when I visited their establishments seeking photographs: Mr Hywel Matthews, archivist at Pontypridd Library; Mr Brian Davies, curator at Pontypridd Museum and his assistant, Mr David Gwyer.

Foreword

Dylan Thomas once mischievously described Swansea as 'a string of villages tied together with gossip'. The same could be said of the urban district of Pontypridd, within which Treforest is normally located. Treforest is not Pontypridd; it is its own place with its own quite distinct character.

When the iron industry began to transform the valley in the early 1800s, a market was established here long before the market in Pontypridd. This was a community of mixed origins, with chapels and churches built for the Welsh, English and Irish who came to work here.

Evidence of Treforest's industrial past is all around us. Coal from the Rhondda crossed the Machine Bridge, the oldest railway viaduct in the world – now to be restored. Forest House, once the home of the Crawshays, is now part of the University of Glamorgan. The first buildings of the tinplate works, long in ruins, are to be refurbished.

Treforest can build a future without destroying all evidence of its past. I am sure that this book will be much appreciated by those who know the area. I hope that it will also help newcomers, especially those at the university, to appreciate the community in which they now work and live.

Brian Davies
Curator, Pontypridd Museum

Introduction

In 1700, Treforest was a beautiful green valley with wooded hills sweeping down to the clear waters of the River Taff. The river, at that time, would have been well stocked with salmon and trout. The small number of inhabitants would have been farmers or farm workers and would have lived in very simple dwellings.

Industrialisation really began in Treforest in 1794 when William Crawshay I (1764-1834) purchased a piece of land at Ynyspenllwch, on which stood a small tin-rolling mill, from Christopher James. The mill was developed and became the Treforest Tin Plate Works, operating until 1946. Since that date, the site has been used by P. Leiner & Son, who ran a a gelatin plant there until 1980, and then by Webb's Timber for some years. The buildings are still standing today, albeit in a very derelict state, and are currently the property of the Welsh Development Agency.

The Lower Treforest Works was set up by William Crawshay II (1788-1867) and managed by his son Francis Crawshay (1811-1878) until 1867, when it was taken over by a consortium. The works ceased production in 1900.

The Taff Vale ironworks, known locally as Y Gwaith Bach, was situated just off the Broadway. Supposedly founded by a group of Westmorland Wesleyans in the eighteenth century, it passed into the Fothergill family in 1860 and closed in around 1900. The Treforest Foundry opened on this site in around 1906 and operated until it was demolished in April 2004.

By 1810, coal was being exported from the lower Rhondda valley and a tramway was constructed from Trehafod to the Machine Bridge at Glyntaff, where the coal was weighed before being loaded onto barges at the Dr Griffiths canal. This canal linked up with the Glamorganshire canal at Dynea in Rhydyfelin.

In August 1811, a market opened in Treforest and it was one of the first in the principality. There was also a hide and wool market near the old slaughterhouse, which was sited near Castle Inn Bridge.

In 1841, the Taff Vale railway was opened, in order to meet the needs of the expanding coal industry in the Valleys. Treforest station opened in around 1846.

Disaster struck the Treforest area in 1849, when an outbreak of cholera claimed the lives of hundreds of inhabitants.

In 1913, the South Wales and Monmouthshire School of Mines was opened in Forest House in Treforest. The school developed over the years and today the school is the famous University of Glamorgan.

In 1936, the Welsh Industrial Estates Corporation decided to build an industrial estate in Treforest because there was a high rate of unemployment in the area, due to the collapse of the coal industry. The estate thrived throughout the war years and, in its heyday, employed 16,000 personnel. Today the estate is still in existence but nearly all of the old companies, which used to be household names, have closed down. Their factories have been demolished and replaced with modern units.

Across the River Taff lies Glyntaff, a town famous for its links with Dr William Price and the fact that it was the site of the first crematorium to be built in Wales.

Today Treforest is mainly a university town with a trading estate. Its short life as a centre of heavy industry was due to the lack of any coal mines in the area and the fact that iron and steel manufacture was transferred to the South Wales coast to be near the docks.

Rhodri John Powell
April 2005

one

Treforest

In 1794, William Crawshay I purchased a small tin mill on the bank of the River Taff at Ynyspenllwch, opposite Rhydyfelin. The mill was developed and operated by the Crawshay family until 1876, when it was sold to a consortium. After years of fluctuating fortunes, the mill finally closed in 1946. The buildings were taken over by P. Leiner & Son, who operated a gelatin plant on the site until 1980. The buildings are now in ruins and are owned by the Welsh Development Agency.

These men worked at the Treforest tinworks when this picture was taken in 1930.

The remains of the Treforest tinworks in 2004.

Another view of the derelict Treforest tinworks in 2004.

The Julia Bridge in 1920. The bridge was named after Francis Crawshay's daughter-in-law. A tramroad over this bridge took the finished tinplate from the tinworks to the Dr Griffiths canal at Rhydyfelin. This canal linked up with the Glamorganshire canal at Dynea.

In 1929, the Julia Bridge was badly damaged when there was extensive flooding in the area. It has now been demolished.

The Forest ironworks was established by Francis Crawshay in the 1850s. When Crawshay retired in 1867, he sold the ironworks to a consortium and it became known as the Forest Iron & Steel Works.

This is another view of the Forest ironworks. It closed in 1900 and today the site is occupied by the University of Glamorgan.

Men at work in the Forest ironworks in around 1900.

The Cold Roll Mill at the Treforest tinworks in around 1920.

This is all that remains of the Taff Vale ironworks, which was known locally as Y Gwaith Bach. The ironworks was supposedly founded in the eighteenth century by a group of Westmorland Wesleyans and was passed on to the Fothergill family in 1860. It closed in around 1900.

A view of the interior of Treforest Foundry, which was opened in 1906 on the site of the old Taff Vale ironworks. The foundry was demolished in April 2004.

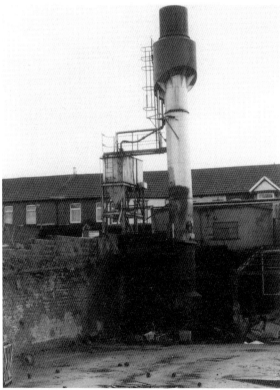

Above: The closure of Treforest Foundry was the end of an era. David Russell started working there when he was fifteen and was an employee for forty-eight years. The foundry was demolished in 2004 and the site is now a private housing estate called Windsor Court.

Left: The furnace at Treforest Foundry was demolished in April 2004.

Francis Crawshay was born in 1811 and was the second son of William Crawshay II. From an early age Francis was rather eccentric and he was sometimes a great worry to his father. He took over the management of the Treforest Works in 1831. He was very popular with the workforce and was the only member of the Crawshay family who spoke Welsh. He was a friend of Dr William Price, the celebrated druid and pioneer of cremation. Francis retired to Sevenoaks in Kent, where he died in 1878. Many streets in Treforest are named after his family. As well as Francis Street, there is Laura Street, which is named after his wife, and Tudor Street and Owen Street, named after his sons.

Left: This obelisk, which stood alongside the old tramroad in front of Castle House, was erected by Francis Crawshay and his brother Henry in 1844. Around the base is the following inscription: 'I am a model of the only obelisk now standing at Heliopolis erected by Osortsen – the earliest of pharaohs.' Today it still stands on the same spot in a small garden.

Below: The tall stones in this neo-druidic circle bore the names and dates of numerous members of the Crawshay family, beginning with William in 1650. The collection was started by Francis Crawshay and there were around twenty of the stones by the time Francis died in 1878. In his will, he instructed his son Tudor to erect them in a circle in the grounds of Forest House. Unfortunately they were removed in the mid-1950s and used in the foundations of the extension to the Glamorgan Technical College.

Forest House was the home of Francis Crawshay and his family. It was originally built by his grandfather on the site of Forest Isaf Farm, which gave its name to the Forest Works. The house had extensive grounds: Llantwit Road and its side streets stand on what used to be its orchards. After the Crawshays, the house was occupied by Walter Morgan, a local solicitor, and in 1913 it became the South Wales and Monmouthshire School of Mines. Today, the house is known as Ty Crawshay.

Before Francis Crawshay and his family moved to Forest House, they lived in Castle House. Today it is a private dwelling.

Left: These children are standing outside a house in Oxford Street in the 1940s.

Below: Treforest children helping in the election campaign of Mr T.J. Mardy Jones in the 1920s. Mardy Jones was the Labour MP for Pontypridd from 1922 to 1935.

H.G. Joshua & Sons of Park Street has been a supplier of ironmongery to the community for over 100 years. This picture shows the store in 1904.

By 1921, H.G. Joshua's store was also selling bicycles. The business is still in the family and is currently run by Mr Lyn Joshua.

Crown Stores in Fothergill Street in 1910. The shop sold groceries and advertised itself as a 'family grocer' and 'provision merchant'.

T. Evans' shop in Park Street, seen here in 1900, was also a grocery.

In 1920, David Williams had a grocer's shop in Park Street.

David Williams' delivery van in around 1920. The store prided itself on offering 'quality and value'.

This shop, photographed in 1930, stood in Cardiff Road, near Castle Inn Bridge. The Victorian hide and wool market was situated at the end of the terraced houses.

The Broadway, Treforest, in around 1900. The tramlines can be seen on the road.

Above left: The site of the Cecil cinema in Fothergill Street. In 1904, the Cecil cinema had a 'cinema hall and shops'. The house was demolished in 1904. *Above right:* Oddfellows Hall in Park Terrace was built in 1848 by one of the many Benevolent Societies that existed at that time. In its early days the hall accommodated many Irish people, who came over to this country during the potato famine. In the Depression it was used as a soup kitchen, and it housed evacuees and American soldiers during the Second World War. Today it is a private dwelling.

The tramlines are visible in this view of Fothergill Street, *c.* 1910. The street was named after Rowland Fothergill (1794-1871), who was the owner of the Taff Vale ironworks.

A.F. Parker's butchers shop was well stocked for Christmas 1930. This is what a traditional butcher's shop used to look like.

A tram travelling along Park Street in 1925. David Williams' grocery can be seen on the right.

The staff of Ceiriog Bakery pose for an official photograph in 1900. The bakery was situated behind the Crown public house, now called the Pick and Shovel Hotel, in Fothergill Street.

Mr and Mrs P. Cottrell ran the Treforest Dairy on the Broadway.

This 1950 view of Treforest shows the old Barry railway station behind Llantwit Road. In the centre is the School of Mines and the circle of Crawshay stones. The stones were buried in the foundations when the college was expanded in the mid-1950s.

Treforest railway station opened in 1847. These children are setting off on an outing in the early 1900s.

Right: Trams were a common sight in Treforest in the early twentieth century. This picture was taken in 1910.

Below: In 1892 it was decided that an English chapel was needed in the area, and the Castle Square chapel was built. Originally known as Ebenezer Hall, it was commenced at Treforest as a daughter church, and the Ebenezer members worshipped there while their church was being re-built. Today it is the Castle Square United Reform church.

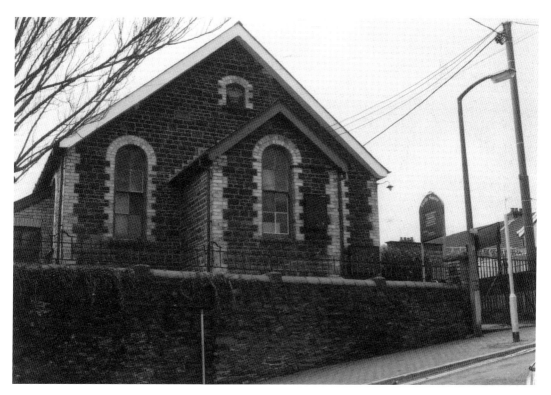

The English Wesleyan Methodist chapel was built in 1852.

The Treforest Wesleyan chapel choir in 1930.

This imposing building is St Dyfrig's Catholic church, which was built in 1926.

Treforest United choir in 1910, with conductor Alun Dummer.

The Libanus chapel is also known as Capel-y-Bedyddwr. It was built in 1846 and stands in Fothergill Street.

At the side of the Libanus chapel is a well-maintained graveyard.

The houses in Long Row originally faced the tinworks tramroad. They were built by William Crawshay to house the workers that he brought down from his Dowlais works. The houses had a catslide roof, a feature common in buildings around the Crawshay works in the nineteenth century.

A cyclone on 27 October 1917 caused serious damage to the houses in Long Row.

Above: The falls near Castle Inn Bridge. The old slaughterhouse can be seen on the right.

Left: A young worker at the Treforest slaughterhouse in around 1930.

The weir across the River Taff, seen here in 1938, was built in 1830 by William Crawshay II, in order to supply water to the Treforest tinworks.

In 1887, Castle Inn Bridge was widened from 13ft to 26ft. The bridge is now a pedestrian way only.

The county police station was built in 1934. During the Second World War the station had around forty special constables. The officer in charge at that time was Police Sergeant Reginald Greening.

The Glamorgan special constabulary Treforest section committee in 1941. From left to right, back row: J.S. Hughes, H. Morgan, O. Mantle, B. Gomer, D.J. Thomas, E.M. Rees. Front row: E.F. Knowles, J.L. Lowman, Police Sergeant R. Greening, B. Egan, A.D. Tromans.

The old Pontypridd to Barry railway line opened in 1889 and ran along the back of Llantwit Road. Today all that remains is the tunnel entrance at the rear of the University of Glamorgan.

This view of the Broadway shows the main Cardiff railway line, the Ford car dealer's forecourt and, in the background, the famous Brown Lennox chainworks. The works closed in 2004 and will shortly be demolished to make way for a supermarket.

The gasworks at Glyntaff are visible in this view from Llantwit Road. It was opened in 1895 and has now been demolished.

Llantwit Road can be seen in this picture, as well as the School of Mines. This was taken before the University of Glamorgan was built. Behind Llantwit Road is the old Pontypridd to Barry railway line. The houses in the foreground are the prefabs in Morien Crescent, which were demolished in the late 1960s.

The Treforest miners' boot repairing centre, set up by the miners during the General Strike in 1926 to repair the boots of miners' children.

Mrs Ada Jones of Kingsland Terrace was a First World War widow. She is seen here with her children: Alice, Albert, Rhys, Lana, Ada and Freda.

Members of the Wood Street Club setting off on an outing to Barry Island in 1936. The working men's club met in a large house with a monkey tree in the front garden.

The residents of King Street held a party for the Coronation of King George VI in 1937 and these little girls took part in the celebrations. From left to right: Cecily Hewlett, Betty Hewlett, Shirley James, Audrey James, Anne Howells, Pat Dowling, Margaret Williams, Rene James, Maureen Cannon and Betty James.

Right: In 1911, Katy, Hilda, Myrtle and Mia Fice lived at No. 91 Broadway. Their parents, Albert and Lavinia Fice, had walked from Devon in 1900 to find work in the local colliery.

Below: Chris Percy, a haulage contractor from Queen Street, and his father took part in the annual Taff Vale Park parade in 1930.

The boy in this photograph is a young Tom Jones. The famous singer was born Thomas Jones Woodward and is seen here with his family. From left to right, back row: his father Tom; cousin Emrys Jones and his wife Betty; his father's sister Sheila; cousin Dorothy Jones and Freda, his mother. Front row: cousins Jean and Ada, sister Margaret and Tom Jones.

Members of the Treforest Park Womens' Guild in the 1950s. They met at the Park Rovers Football Club hut.

The Band of Hope carnival took place in Castle Street on 21 April 1925. The Band of Hope was a national temperance organisation that organised activities for children.

Members of the Treforest Toc H in the 1930s. Toc H is a charitable organisation that began during the First World War.

In 1953 residents of the Broadway held a tea party to celebrate the Coronation of Queen Elizabeth II.

The Broadway residents posed for a photograph outside the entrance to Taff Vale Park to mark the occasion.

Treforest residents waiting for the tram in Park Street in 1906.

This was Windsor Road in the 1930s. In the background are the famous Round Towers built by Dr William Price.

The Treforest football club in the 1887/88 season.

The Treforest Mission AFC in around 1920. The team seems to have had a successful season.

The football fields were created when the White Tips – the waste from the ironworks above Duke Street – were levelled in 1930. The White Tips are visible in this view of Treforest, taken from Glyntaff.

These are the workmen who levelled the White Tips to make the football fields.

Park Rovers football club distributed Christmas gifts in 1930.

Park Rovers football club in the 1931/32 season.

Members of Park Rovers football club in 1939, seen here on the converted old White Tips, including Tommy Booth, Frank Batton, Jackie Booth, Eddie Jones, County Councillor Gladys Williams and Patsie Casey.

The Park Rovers football club committee members in 1950.

Members of Park Rovers football club in 1950. The remnants of the old White Tips are visible in the background.

Park Rovers football club in 1967. From left to right, back row: D. Morgan, R. Thomas, S. Burgwyn, J. Legge, G. Stacey, C. Tritchler, J. Batton, A. Hughes, P. Stephens, M. Booth, C. Rickards. Front row: J. Casey, P. Brennan, D. Stacey, C. Granelli, B. Casey. The Park Rovers clubhouse was destroyed by fire in 1974.

Another local football club was Treforest Corries, seen here in the 1922/23 season.

In the 1923/24 season, Treforest Labour football club won the Greyhound Cup and were runners-up in the Pontypridd and District League.

These players were members of Park Guild football club in 1947.

The Park Guild football club players posed for an official photograph in 1949.

Treforest also had a women's football team, called Treforest Ladies. These women were the team in 1950.

This was the Treforest Ladies charity football team in 1952.

Above: Treforest Primary School opened in 1875. The school was originally the Treforest Board School, which opened in the Calvary Baptist chapel schoolroom on 3 June 1872.

Left: Mrs Sarah Rhoderick was the headmistress of Treforest Primary School in 1916.

The children of Treforest Primary School in fancy dress in around 1900.

Headmaster Mr Davies and teacher Mrs Adams pose with their pupils at Treforest Primary School in 1957.

Calvary English Baptist chapel was built in 1851. In 1870, the government passed the Education Act which called for the setting up of locally elected school boards, who received funding dependent on performance. These education establishments were referred to as Board Schools. Treforest Board School, which had accommodation for 100 pupils, came into existence in this chapel on the 3 June 1872, with Mr Evan Watkin as the teacher. In August 1875, the pupils were transferred to the new Board School which later became Treforest Primary School.

The children of Treforest Primary School had a Christmas party in 1954.

St Michael's Roman Catholic Junior School was built in 1970.

Treforest Gospel Hall is situated on the Broadway.

Races were held at Taff Vale Park. The track is lined with spectators watching the races in 1910.

These were the competitors in the Welsh Sprint Handicap race held at Taff Vale Park in 1909. The man on the far left is the referee and the race was won by Mr Holloway, standing third from the right.

There used to be a cycle track in Taff Vale Park but it was demolished in around 1930.

This cycle race took place at the Taff Vale Park track in around 1910.

The 1st and 2nd Treforest Scout troops in 1918.

The Pontypridd Dragons football team at Taff Vale Park in 1930.

Councillor Roper, standing to the left of the child in the centre, officially opened the Treforest tennis courts in 1930.

The railway bridge over the Broadway was reconstructed in 1938. The bridge was removed in 1969.

Madam Muriel Jones's choir was founded in 1927. The members sang before royalty on around twenty occasions.

Madam Muriel Jones's choir at Treforest, just before they went to Windsor to sing before the Duke and Duchess of York and the Princesses in April 1935.

Above left: Saron Methodist church was built in 1890. *Above right:* The Otley Arms, which was originally the Forest Commercial Inn, was built in 1860. This public house came into the Otley family in 1975 when it was purchased by Mr Alfred Otley. At that time he was steward of the Student Union bar at the Polytechnic of Wales.

The Treforest Constitutional Club is now the Broadway Social Club. The Co-op store next door became a glazier's shop in the 1970s. It later became a security equipment store and today it is Advanced Crusher Spares.

The Rickards Arms in Park Street has been serving the community for over 125 years.

The Forest Hotel was once an important meeting place for sporting enthusiasts. There used to be two wells near this public house that supplied the local residents with their water.

Furniture removers Len and John Preece celebrated fifty years of business in 1977. Len Preece set up the business in 1927 when he purchased his first lorry for £7 10s. In 1972 Len retired at the age of seventy-two and his son John took over the business. John continued until April 2004, when the business was wound up after seventy-seven years of service to the community.

As well as running the family removal business, John Preece was mayor of Pontypridd Town Council from 1984 to 1985. He is seen here with his wife Ann at his Civic Service in Saron chapel in Treforest in June 1984.

The former Dan-y-Graig Hotel became the home of the world famous Groggs – hand-sculpted figurines of celebrities – in 1971, when Mr John Hughes and his family moved here from Llantwit Road.

The stars look down on John Hughes (far right), his son Richard (far left), his daughter Catherine (second from right) and Pat, the manageress (second from left).

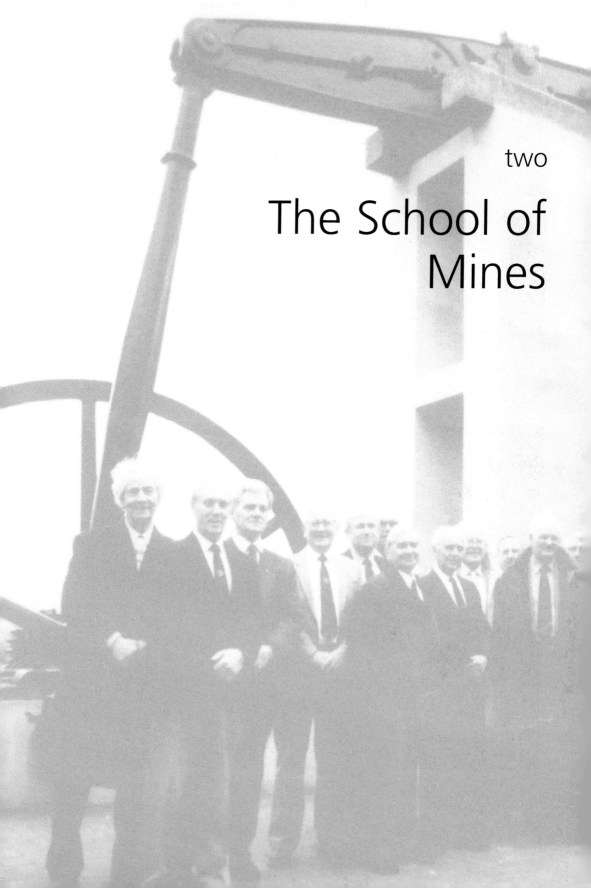

two

The School of
Mines

As a result of the rapid expansion of the South Wales coalfields in the early 1900s, the coal owners recognised that there was a need to train and educate workers in order to improve efficiency and reduce the human suffering associated with coal mining.

In 1908, several of the principal coal owners in South Wales and Monmouthshire agreed that there was a need for an educational establishment for young men intending to make a career in the mining profession. Several meetings took place over the years and on 30 March 1911 a circular was sent out to all coal owners in South Wales and Monmouthshire recommending the setting up of a School of Mines.

In 1912, the financial backing was agreed by the coal owners and the School of Mines was established at Forest House in Treforest. The house was purchased from the widow of the late Mr Walter Morgan, a local solicitor. The layout of the proposed school included mining, electrical and mechanical laboratories, a chemical laboratory, a physics laboratory, a drawing office and an administration office.

On 17 January 1913, Professor George Knox was appointed Director of Mining and Mr John Samuel his deputy. The South Wales and Monmouthshire School of Mines opened in October 1913 with 30 full-time and 110 part-time students. Expansion was rapid and new courses were introduced to meet the requirements of the coal industry and also the increasing number of students.

Unfortunately, following the devastating effect of the 1926 General Strike, the board of governors of the school found it difficult to continue funding the establishment. As a result of these financial difficulties, the board of governors agreed that the School of Mines should be handed over to Glamorgan County Council. The transfer deed was signed on 11 February 1929.

The school remained open during the Second World War, although the number of students obviously decreased. At this time, the school had its own Officer Cadet Corps.

Further changes have taken place over the years. In 1940 the School of Mines became the School of Mines and Technology. It became the Glamorgan Technical College in 1949 and then the Glamorgan College of Technology in 1958. In 1970 it became Glamorgan Polytechnic and two years later it combined with the Barry College of Education and became the Polytechnic of Wales. It became the University of Glamorgan in 1992 and today, as a modern forward-thinking university, it offers over 200 courses to students from all over the world.

The School of Mines was opened in Forest House in 1913.

This view of Forest Road, taken in around 1920, shows the School of Mines.

Forest House is now called Ty Crawshay. The house was the original School of Mines but is now part of the University of Glamorgan, housing the School of Humanities and Social Science.

This is a side view of Ty Crawshay.

In 1934, a celebration was held to commemorate the twenty-first anniversary of the opening of the South Wales and Monmouthshire School of Mines. The school was taken over by Glamorgan County Council in 1929.

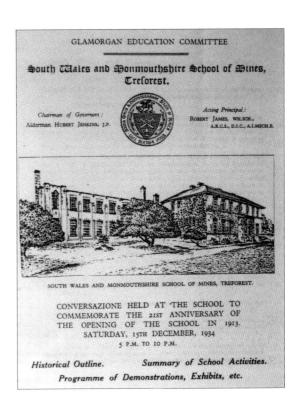

This was the floor layout of the School of Mines in 1934.

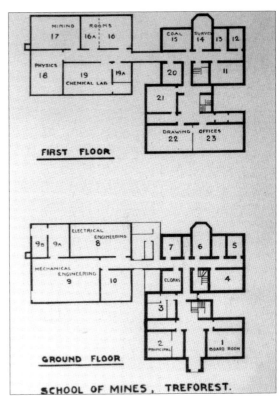

This winding and pumping beam engine, which was designed by John Calvert in 1845, was removed from Gelliwion colliery and erected in the grounds of the School of Mines.

Forest Road in around 1910. Forest House can be seen at the end of the road.

In the 1926/27 academic year, these young men were members of the Student Representative Council at the School of Mines.

The Foundry Class at the School of Mines and Technology in April 1941.

The Officer Cadet Force at the School of Mines, seen here in 1942, consisted of full-time and part-time students. The Commanding Officer was Major Watkins, who was head of chemistry at the school.

The Pontypridd 2nd Battalion of the Home Guard in the grounds of the School of Mines in May 1941.

A meeting of ex-senior staff and principals of the school in 1970. From left to right, standing: Roy Greening, John Davies, Tom Davies. Seated: D.P. Evans, John Cotter, Aerwen James. On the back wall are framed pictures of Professor George Knox, the first principal of the School of Mines (left) and Professor Robert James (right).

Members of the Department of Mechanical and Production Engineering in the 1960s.

Former members of staff and students of the Mining Department in front of John Calvert's beam engine.

Llantwit Road was built on land that was originally the orchards of Forest House. The house with the round tower is now the Academic Office of the university and the house next to it is the Human Resources Department.

HND mechanical engineering students in 1963.

LLB graduates in 1983. The author's daughter Siân, second from right, is now a commercial lawyer in Cardiff.

The main entrance of the University of Glamorgan.

The Glyntaff site of the University of Glamorgan houses the Law School, the School of Care Science and the Welsh Institute of Health and Social Care. The site used to be the Pontypridd Urban District Council's tram and bus depot.

three

Treforest
Industrial
Estate

The Treforest Industrial Estate came into being in July 1936 when the site was chosen by the Welsh Industrial Estates Corporation, a body which was superseded by the Welsh Development Agency in 1974. The creation of an industrial estate was an attempt to try and eleviate the unemployment in the area following the collapse of the coal industry and the Depression of the 1930s.

The original site covered 165 acres and allowed space for gardens and recreation grounds in addition to factories. It was intended to preserve the existing rural community as far as possible.

Three factories were completed by 1937 and employed sixty-nine people. By 1938 the number of factories had increased to eleven. Considerable expansion took place during the Second World War and by 1944 the estate employed 16,000 personnel in 1 million square feet of factory space. The end of the war saw the release of requisitioned space and the return of a number of firms which had previously moved from the estate.

By the 1960s around sixty-two firms were operating on the industrial estate. In the 1970s there were around forty-nine companies occupying units.

This chapter includes photographs of some of the companies who occupied these factory units, none of which are now operating on the estate. Today, these old factory units have been replaced with modern units and the number of workers currently employed is a fraction of the number employed in the heyday of the estate.

Opposite above: Construction of the industrial estate in around 1936.

Opposite below: Workmen at the industrial estate site in 1936.

In the 1970s this was the office of the Welsh Development Agency. The agency was responsible for leasing factories on the estate. At this time there were forty-nine companies occupying units.

Wire Products (Wales) Ltd specialised in steel sheet-metal products, wire products and metal fabrication.

The Glamorgan County Council Workshop for the Blind manufactured knitted goods, baskets, mats and brushes and carried out chair recaning.

South Wales Switchgear Ltd were manufacturers of electrical switchgear, power transformers and domestic appliances.

Standard Telephone & Cable Ltd was a telecommunication engineering company.

Firth Cleveland made sintered products and fastenings.

General Music Strings Ltd manufactured musical instrument strings from gut, nylon and all kinds of metals.

This was the factory of Estate Printers Ltd.

P. Leiner & Sons Ltd made industrial and edible gelatins.

The storage tanks of P. Leiner & Sons Ltd, with a delivery tanker loading gelatins.

ITT Creed Ltd produced high-speed telegraph and telephone equipment.

The Mid Glamorgan County Council Training and Work Centre.

The Skillcentre was a government training centre, retraining unemployed people to give them the skills required to work in industry.

The Ford Motor Company manufactured spark plugs and ignition equipment.

Copigraph Ltd were manufacturers of carbon paper, typewriter ribbons, writing inks and office paste, and were wholesale and retail stationers.

Neptune Brass & Aluminium Co. Ltd produced non-ferrous sand and gravity die castings, shell mouldings and hot brass and copper pressings.

Pearl Paints Ltd.

Northgate Group Ltd manufactured children's clothes.

Aero Zipp Ltd manufactured zips and fasteners.

Western Board Mills Ltd.

The demolition of the South Wales Electrical Power Company's coal-fired generating station at Upper Boat. It was opened in 1908 and was out of use by 1973.

Shalibane Ltd were manufacturers of fasteners and allied products.

four

Glyntaff

Treforest and Glyntaff were rural communities in the mid-nineteenth century.

Machine Bridge was built by Dr Richard Griffiths in 1809 to link his tramroad from the Broadway to his private canal. This canal ran from Glyntaff to Dynea in Rhydyfelin, where it joined the Glamorgan canal. There was a weighing machine at one end of the bridge to weigh the drams of coal.

St Mary's church was built in 1839. The old schoolrooms can be seen in the foreground. This photograph must have been taken before 27 October 1913 because on that day the spire was damaged when a tornado hit the village and it was never replaced.

The tornado in October 1913 caused extensive damage to the vicarage of St Mary's church.

The tramlines being laid over Canal Bridge in Glyntaff in 1903. St Mary's church, complete with spire, is visible in the background.

Local residents review the damage caused by the 1913 tornado.

This winter scene is Glyntaff Cutting in around 1900.

The residents of Glyntaff gather to watch a wedding at St Mary's church in around 1900.

The Brown Lennox Chainworks Mission Hall in Ynysynghared Road was built in 1873 and is now a private house.

The Glamorganshire canal at Glyntaff in around 1910, with the Mission Hall in the background.

Canal Cottages in Nightingale's Bush, Glyntaff, stand alongside the towpath of the old Glamorganshire canal.

The Glamorganshire canal at Glyntaff is in a neglected state today.

The Duke of Bridgewater Arms, known as the Old Duke, used to be one of the most famous inns of the nineteenth century. It was here that the stagecoaches and mail coaches travelling between Cardiff and Merthyr changed horses. It was demolished in 1969 when the A470 was constructed.

The Glamorganshire canal at Glyntaff in 1950. On the right is the Farmers Arms Hotel, which was also demolished to make way for the A470.

Dr William Price was born on 4 March 1800 in the parish of Rudry. When he was thirteen years old he was apprenticed to Evan Morgan, a surgeon practising in the Caerphilly area. Later he went to London to further his medical studies and, in 1821, became a member of the Royal College of Surgeons. He returned to Wales and practised in the Pontypridd, Treforest and Llantrisant areas and had a surgery at Gellifelig in Glyntaff. He was also physician to the Crawshay family and a personal friend of Francis Crawshay.

Price was a rather eccentric man and a practising druid, who was often seen wearing a foxskin hat. He will always be remembered for introducing cremation to Wales. On 13 January 1884, he attempted to cremate the body of his baby son Iesu Grist at East Caerlan in Llantisant. This action resulted in his arrest and trial but he was acquitted. He died on 23 January 1893 and was cremated at East Caerlan on 31 January 1893. A stained-glass window was installed in the North Chapel at Glyntaff crematorium as a memorial to him.

In 1860 Dr William Price designed and commenced the building of these Round Houses in Glyntaff. They were intended to form the entrance to a mansion that he planned to build. Unfortunately, the mansion was never built due to a dispute with Lady Llanover, a major landowner at that time.

The Round Houses in the 1950s. They are still standing today and are private residences.

Graig-Yr-Helfa can be seen in the foreground. The large detached house behind the terraced houses is Oak House, which used to be known as Gellifelig. It was the home and surgery of Dr William Price. All these houses were demolished in around 1964 to make way for fifty-eight new houses. The house in the background is Hillside View.

Machine Bridge and Glyntaff Bridge in around 1920.

The Duke of Bridgewater Arms, with the Glamorganshire canal in the foreground.

The Glyntaff cemetery opened in 1875. In 1924, the existing chapel building was adapted and became the first crematorium in Wales, and the sixteenth in Great Britain. The crematorium has links with Dr William Price, who lived in Pontypridd and was active in establishing cremation in 1884. In 1966, a stained-glass window was fitted in the North Chapel as a memorial to Dr Price.

John Bradshaw of Pontypridd died on 31 May 1875. His was the first body to be interred in Glyntaff cemetery.

The Pontypridd Burial Board in August 1902. From left to right, back row: Richard Rees, Frederick Judd, James Spickett, F.G. Edwards, William Jones, P. Gowan, Morgan Rees, D.J. James. Front row: R. Gwyngyll Hughes, James Roberts, Richard Rogers, Henry Mills, M. Jenkins.

The construction of the Garden of Rest at Glyntaff crematorium in 1956.

The interior of the South Chapel at Glyntaff crematorium in 1950.

The Garden of Rest at Glyntaff crematorium was officially opened on 20 July 1957 by Councillor H. Gardner, chairman of the Pontyridd Burial Board and Cremation Authority. Mr T. Howard Burt, the Superintendent Registrar, was also present.

Left: The obelisk in the graveyard of St Mary's church in Glyntaff marks the grave of Richard Crawshay, the second son of Francis and Laura Crawshay. He was born on 24 May 1847 but lived for less than a year, dying on 2 April 1848. The obelisk bears the inscription: 'Suffer little children to come unto me'. It was this inscription that allowed this 'pagan' edifice to be erected in the churchyard.

Below: The Sunday School class at St Mary's church in 1916, with Revd Gomer Jones seated centre.

The old Pontypridd Urban District Council Transport Offices and bus depot were demolished and the site taken over by the University of Glamorgan.

The craftsmen in the Glyntaff Tram Department in 1923.

The Pontypridd and Rhondda Tramway Company first operated a line in Pontypridd town in 1885 and in 1905 the system was electrified. The staff of the tramway company posed with one of the trams at Glyntaff in 1910.

Trolley buses were introduced in the area in 1931 and remained in service until 1957.

Right: A tram went through the side of the tram shed at the Glyntaff depot in 1910.

Below: The Columbarium building at Glyntaff crematorium was built in 1932. In this building, cremated remains can be placed in a niche, as an alternative to scattering or burial. If relatives wish, a memorial can be placed over the niche.

The Girls' Grammar School was originally the Girls' Intermediate School, which was opened on 15 September 1913 and had accommodation for 200 pupils. The pupils were transferred to the new comprehensive school and today the building is the Glamorgan Centre for Art and Design Technology.

Lock Cottage is situated by the Glamorganshire canal at Glyntaff.

five

Rhydyfelin

These roadsweepers are about to commence cleaning Cardiff Road in 1910.

Another view of Cardiff Road in 1910, with a draper's shop on the left.

This was the first passenger coach on the Rhydyfelin–Cardiff railway line in 1908. The line was constructed by the Cardiff Railway Company. They intended to extend the line to Pontypridd but this section was never completed because of opposition from other railway companies operating in the area.

The Hawthorn Inn in Rhydyfelin in 1910.

The Glamorganshire canal ran from Merthyr Tydfil to Cardiff and was built to transport iron to the docks. It was 25 miles long and had a drop of approximately 560ft, which required fifty-two locks. Work commenced on the construction in 1790, funded by the Crawshay family and some of the other Merthyr ironmasters. The section between Merthyr and Pontypridd was completed in 1792 and the section to Cardiff by 1794.

The Glamorganshire canal at Rhydyfelin. The canal remained in operation until around 1898.

Lock Lewis on the Glamorganshire canal at Rhydyfelin in around 1910. The barges operating on this canal were flat-bottomed. They were approximately 60ft long, 9ft wide and carried around 5 tons of iron.

Dynea Lock on the Glamorganshire canal in 1920.

On 19 October 1908 the Glamorganshire canal burst its banks and caused damage to properties in Dynea.

A further view of the damage caused at Dynea when the canal burst its banks in October 1908.

A coach trip about to depart from outside the New Inn in 1910.

The children in this Sunday School procession in Cardiff Road in 1930 are on their way to a tea party.

Ebenezer chapel and Cardiff Road, *c.* 1950. These buildings were all demolished in 1969 to make way for the A470.

Ebenezer chapel was built in 1846 and rebuilt in 1896 to accommodate the increased membership. The chapel had its origins at Ynys Farm in Ebenezer Street, the home of Mr Evan Morgan, where services were held on Sundays. The chapel was demolished in 1969 when the A470 was constructed. The gravestones were removed and placed in Glyntaff cemetery.

The deacons of Ebenezer chapel in 1903. From left to right, back row: David Williams, Evan Davies, Benjamin Jones, Evan John, John Jones. Front row: Henry Roberts, Ivor Williams, Parch D.G. Evans, Samuel Jones, John Edwards.

The Deacons of Ebenezer chapel in 1960. From left to right, back row: W.J. Lloyd, D.B. Williams, G. Edwards, W.J. Edwards. Front row: R. Edwards, Revd Peter J. Lewis, Henry Davies.

The Round Houses at Rhydyfelin, seen here in 1936, stood on the site now occupied by Pontypridd College. They were built in around 1850 by Francis Crawshay and were demolished in 1938. There are two rumours about why these houses were built: some people say that the circular design was to stop housewives gossiping on the doorsteps; others say that Francis Crawshay had a bet with his brother Henry over who could build eight houses on the smallest piece of land.

The back view of the Round Houses. It is stated that in the centre courtyard of these houses was a large tree stump, whose roots probably acted as a drain for rainwater.

Residents of the Round Houses with the local ice-cream man in 1936.

Duffryn Street in the 1930s.

Colonel Henry Morgan Lindsey unveiled the war memorial at St Luke's church on 14 June 1923. The memorial was erected by the inhabitants of Rhydyfelin and district.

Pwll-Y-Gwiad Farm once stood on the site of Ebenezer Street. It was the home of Mr Evan Thomas and his family.

Rhydyfelin Wanderers amateur football club in the 1922/23 season.

The old Co-op store was built in 1929.

This bus crashed in Cardiff Road in the 1950s.

The junction of Duffryn Road and Cardiff Road in around 1950.

The Duffryn Arms was known locally as the Duff. The adjacent building used to be a pharmacy.

The Duffryn Arms has been renovated and is now called the Rhydyfelin Arms.

Other local titles published by Tempus

Rhiwbina
KEN GRAHAM AND JIM TAVERNER

This collection of over 190 postcards and photographs, many never before published, offers a nostalgic glimpse into the history of Rhiwbina during the last century. The book traces the town's growth from a rural village to a modern suburb of the city of Cardiff and highlights important events that have occurred in the area. Aspects of everyday life are also featured, from schools and churches to shops and leisure pursuits.
0 7524 3299 0

Rhondda Revisited
EMRYS JENKINS AND ROY GREEN

Illustrated with over 200 photographs, this third collection of images offers a nostalgic glimpse into the history of the Rhondda Valley during the last century. Many aspects of everyday life are featured, from the buses that took workers to Alfred Polikoff's factory to the local sporting derbies between Treherbert and Treorchy. The book gives an insight into the lives of the people who have proudly called this region their home.
0 7524 3388 1

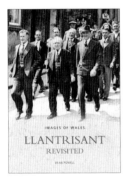

Llantrisant Revisited
DEAN POWELL

This fascinating collection of over 200 old images pays tribute to the people who have proudly called Llantrisant their home. Commanding an outstanding setting on the crest of a hill, Llantrisant's splendour lies in its enchanting beauty and celebrated past. Bloodthirsty battles, pioneering acts of cremation and captured kings of England have all played a part in shaping the town, as have the generations of families who have lived here.
7524 3216 8

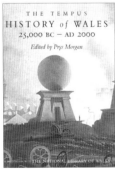

The Tempus History of Wales
PRYS MORGAN

Wales was at the heart of the Industrial Revolution, with towns like Merthyr Tydfil driving the engine of the British Empire. The cultural and social divide between modern, industrialised Wales and the traditional agricultural areas is explored within this comprehensive volume.
0 7524 1983 8

If you are interested in purchasing other books published by Tempus, or in case you have difficulty finding any Tempus books in your local bookshop, you can also place orders directly through our website

www.tempus-publishing.com